THINGS TO DO NOW THAT YOU'RE...A MOM

things to do now

ELFRÉA LOCKLEY   Illustrations by Robyn Neild

that you're...
a mom

spruce

contents

introduction

When we give birth, we move from being women to mothers, and our worlds change in tandem with this transformation. Our eyes are opened to new sights; we see things through the eyes of our newborn babies, and we view ourselves and the world around us very differently. There are few mothers who don't stare in amazement at their babies, awestruck by the beauty and wonder of new life and the miracle of birth. In many ways, the new lives we have created provide us with new lives of our own, and we can bask in the pleasure of recreating ourselves, while giving our newborns the best possible start in life. We are the holders of their

THINGS TO DO NOW THAT YOU'RE...A MOM

memories, their guiding stars, their source of nurturing and unconditional love, and for many, many years the most important people in their lives. This is both a responsibility and an honor, and there are few women who don't rise to the challenge of giving everything they have and are to offer their children the world.

From the sleepy hours after birth, we move into days and weeks where time loses its meaning, and the development of our babies defines our world. As they learn to focus, reach out, and smile, so we learn to find our place in the world—in our new role as mothers. When they roll over, sit up, and take their first tentative steps, we cheer them on, always adapting to their changing needs and our own changing lives. We change as they do, and as we set out on this journey, we may find that we learn more about ourselves, and become more capable, more in tune with our needs as well as those of our babies. Anything and everything is possible, once you've created a new life.

This book is a treasure trove of things that, you, as a new mother, can do—a guide to inspire you as you embark upon the most rewarding adventure of your life.

THINGS TO DO NOW THAT YOU'RE...A MOM

Having a baby may change your life, but it doesn't need to limit it. Motherhood can present the most exciting opportunity for new experiences, trying things you never knew were possible, and, above all, forming a relationship with the most wonderful new friend you could ever have imagined. This book will show you how.

There's no doubt that motherhood can be tiring and challenging at times, but it is also possible to feel stimulated and energized— sharing your life in different ways, and taking the time to get to know yourself and your own needs alongside those of your growing baby. For this reason, you'll find here a bundle of

ideas for activities to keep you on your toes,
explore your creativity, challenge, motivate
and encourage you, help you wind down, and,
better still, do something outrageous—just
because you can. So instead of feeling that
your world has been turned upside down, turn
the world on its head instead, and revel in the
joy of your new life as a mom. Replace what
you miss with equally stimulating pursuits. Be
prepared to test yourself, and push yourself
that little bit further to create the life you've
always wanted. Take some time for reflection
and take off your watch to enjoy the fresh
innocence of your baby and the feelings that
being a mother inspire in you. Find pleasure in
the everyday and in the comfort of being

adored by your baby. And when the feeling strikes, join together with a group of other mothers and get out there and paint the town (baby) pink or blue!

There will be days when you'll bask in serenity and cherish being at home with your baby, and times when exhaustion overwhelms you. Use these moments to restore your sense of calm, and nurture your mind and body. The very best mothers look after themselves, too, so make yourself a priority. You'll find many ways to do just that in this book.

Sing, dance, laugh, share, love, and, above all, celebrate. This book is for you.

new beginnings

"Mom," "Mommy," or "Momma"? Have you thought about what you would like to be called by your new baby? The origin of the word "Mom" is Middle English, to imitate the sound made with closed lips. Welcome yourself, as a new Mom, with a gentle "mmm."

There are many beautiful words to discover from around the world meaning "mother" or "baby." In Hawaiian, "mother" is "makuahine" and "baby" is "kama." In Swahili, the word for infant is "maliaka" and a mother is "mzaa." Unfamiliar words, perhaps, but still difficult to say without a smile. Try them out.

It's no surprise that everything feels different. When we give birth, we are as newborn as our babies. Relish this feeling, and enjoy seeing the world with new eyes.

Now that you share a connection with mothers around the world, learn lullabies from different countries to celebrate this universal bond.

As a woman you are a wonder. Although you might not have realized it before, all moms are truly superheroes. In small ways, you'll notice some superpowers——a new sensitivity to the tiniest sounds, for example. Contemplate all the things you can do now that you've never been able to do before.

I feel whole at last.

MEG MATTHEWS

Some cultures insist new mothers shouldn't leave the house for 28 days, but if you feel like showing your new baby to the world straightaway, don't let anyone stop you. Maybe you need a little more time on your own. Wait until you feel ready.

This is your special time to get to know your baby. Too many visitors can feel exhausting, so find the courage to say "no" to acquaintances. Switch on your answerphone and screen your calls; there is no obligation to speak to anyone in these precious first few days.

Keep your face close to your newborn when you talk, sing, and smile. Very close up (about 8 to 10 inches), your baby has amazing vision; beyond this, her world is blurry. Let her get to know you with crystal clear vision.

Being a Mom allows you to rediscover your own inner child. Relish the time spent blowing raspberries or bouncing your baby in the air. Laugh and play to your heart's content.

When you find that inner child, remember that giggling is a great way to burn calories and relieve tension.

Go fly a kite, up to the highest height, and send all your wishes and dreams about being a mom high up into the air.

Although you may have no time for anyone else but your new baby, remember to register the birth!

Becoming a Mom is an achievement in itself, but if there is another job or occupation you've always aspired to, write this in the "Mother's Occupation" box at the registry office and set a target to achieve this goal in the coming years.

There is so much to remember in the early days. Find a special box for your baby's birth certificate and anything else you want to keep, so that you'll always know where to find them.

Enjoy sleeping on your tummy after many months of life with a bump. You may have to wait a little longer if you are breastfeeding!

Buy yourself a pretty nursing bra. That new cleavage won't last forever!

Cover your bed with luxurious cushions and bed linen to create an extra special place to relax, or feed your baby. Indulgence is the key word!

Close your eyes and marvel at the silky softness of your baby's skin as you stroke him. Nothing compares...

Draw a spiral or any other geometric shapes on card in bold black and white and cut them out to make a mobile. It's still a question of debate whether babies can distinguish colors, but we do know they are drawn to high-contrast images.

Think about asking your hospital or midwife if you can keep your placenta and bury it. This is an old custom that dedicates the placenta back to the earth, in honor of your new baby, and all your body has been through. Wait a year, and then plant a tree or flower. You'll need to wait, or the nutrient-rich placenta will kill your fledgling tribute!

There is no definitive "how to" guide or rulebook for being a mom, so learn to trust your instincts.

Breathe in the magical smell of a new baby—could you ever find the words to describe it?

Don't expect too much from yourself in the early days; remember, you have just given birth, which is an achievement in itself.

There is nothing more wonderful than motherhood and no one will ever love you as much as a small child.

NICOLA HORLICK

Why not try massaging your baby? Not only does it create a great bond between you and your newborn, but it can also be beneficial for your baby's physical and emotional health.

Rearrange your priorities, and shorten your "to-do" list. If you get even one thing done in the first few weeks and months, you've done well.

Sometimes motherhood can be isolating, so join a local baby group, and keep up regular conversations with old friends. They may not share your passion for your new baby, but they'll keep you in touch with the outside world.

Find ways to nurture yourself after giving birth, such as candy, flowers, or even settling down to watch a movie. Simple pleasures can feel extra special, especially when you are breastfeeding.

One of the biggest pleasures in life is simply gazing at your sleeping child. Capture this perfect moment with a photo if you can.

Let things go a little. Take pride in the fact that you are doing one of the most important jobs in the world.

Smile at other mothers you see, even if you don't know them. They might be having a difficult day, or simply enjoy sharing the bond of motherhood.

Moms deserve the best. Buy the most expensive jar of hot chocolate you can find—a cozy treat with an instant feel-good factor. If you are breastfeeding and want to cut down the caffeine, try a cup of hot milk in which you've steeped a vanilla bean. Sprinkle with chocolate shavings or nutmeg, and enjoy.

Buy a newspaper and the number one single from the day on which your baby was born, and tuck it away. When he's older, he'll love to know what the world was like on the day he was born.

If you feel overwhelmed by the sheer number of new emotions that sweep over you, take some time to let them out. Every now and then put your baby into a cot or buggy, and go outside to release with a big shout or scream. Otherwise, turn up the music and dance them off in the kitchen.

It's just fine to admit that there are some things that you don't know about being a mom. Ask questions, and learn from your mistakes. No one gets it right, even second, third, or fourth time round!

Babies cry to communicate something. Tune into your instincts and learn to distinguish your baby's different cries. Sometimes she just may want to be held.

A smile releases feel-good endorphins and is one of the first expressions your baby will mimic, so spend as much time as you can smiling at her.

There are few things as precious as feeling your baby's tiny hands curling around your finger.

Don't feel guilty if it takes an hour or more to get up and dressed, and remember that there is nothing in the rulebook that says you can't spend your day in pajamas. Be gentle with yourself in the early days, and bask in the joy of getting to know your new child.

Is your ironing really necessary? You do so much as a mom and there are bound to be some jobs that don't really need your time and attention. Call in some extra help, and don't be embarrassed about needing it!

Motherhood: All love begins and ends there.

ROBERT BROWNING

Turn early mornings with a baby into something beautiful —open the curtains and watch the sunrise together.

Burning scented candles is a simple way to create a sense of luxury when you feel the urge to be a decadent mother. Turn down the lights, and enjoy the sensual experience of nurturing your new baby.

Stare out of a window as your baby feeds, and let your mind wander. Enjoy the stillness and peace.

If you crave a bit of mental stimulation, do a crossword or sudoku while you give your baby a feed. Get a small-format book that sits neatly on the arm of your chair.

Don't worry about not having time to read books as a new mom. Sometimes magazines or newspapers are all you can manage. If you feel you need a little more stimulation, why not re-read your old childhood favorites? One day soon you'll have the opportunity to introduce them.

Try a face stretch, which is easy to do while you are feeding baby. Scrunch up your face and let it relax slowly. This will help to tone your face as you slowly lose your pregnancy weight.

Turn feeding times into a treat for yourself and invest in a foot-spa, or simply soak your feet in warm water and a few drops of an essential oil. Lavender is a good choice for relaxation, or try ylang-ylang if you want something more sensual.

Ask someone to run you a warm, deep bath as the perfect way to round off a busy day with a baby. If you are on your own, make it a little cooler and share the experience with your newborn.

Breastfeeding in public can be a sensitive issue. If you catch someone watching, surprise them with a remark such as, "Yes, I've got a beautiful baby."

Lavender essential oil is safe to use around infants, so place a few drops in a bath or vaporizer to help you to relax and unwind. Add a drop or two to her baby bath, too. A new study found that babies who bathe with lavender oil are more relaxed, engage more with their parents, and hold eye contact for longer.

Drinking raspberry leaf tea in the weeks following birth can help to help to tone your womb and shrink it back to its normal pre-pregnancy size.

Vacuum while your baby is sleeping. Vacuums produce something called "white noise," which often soothes even the crankiest baby off to sleep. What's more, if they get used to background noise early on, they will learn to sleep through it.

A cup of chamomile tea is an easy, gentle way to instill a sense of calm as you find your feet as a new mom. In the summer months, you can chill it and add a few sprigs of mint for refreshing relaxation.

As a new mom, you'll need to keep your energy levels up. It's often easier to eat smaller meals, regularly throughout the day, to keep your blood sugar stable. This is particularly important if you are breastfeeding. Eating seeds, nuts, wholegrains, and light proteins, such as cheese, milk, and lean turkey or ham, can help to prevent those dips that leave you fighting to keep your eyes open.

It doesn't need to be a chore to keep your iron levels topped up. Indulge in bite-size, energy-boosting snacks like dried fruit (apricots are particularly good), crunchy broccoli with a delicious dip, or even a few squares of decadent bittersweet chocolate.

Remember how important you are too, even when you are giving everything to your baby. Take time to look after yourself, even it is just calling a friend for cover while you take a quiet walk or get your nails painted.

Breastfeeding is thirsty business! Stock up on exotic cordials and fruit juices to combat dehydration and give yourself a little treat!

Indulge your taste buds and have fun experimenting with nutritious snacks for moms to eat on the go. Staying healthy doesn't mean hours in the kitchen. Keep some fresh fruit and crudités to hand, some yummy dips, nuts, seeds, and granola bars that can quickly be decanted into pots for when you are out and about. Make a vat of soup when baby is sleeping and freeze it in small containers to reheat when you need something warm and nourishing.

With a little nontoxic fingerpaint, use your baby's handprint to create perfect thank-you cards for all the gifts you have received. Save a few in your memory box to remember how small everything really was!

Fill your pantry with an exciting range of herbal teas, and keep some honey, lemon, and even a splash of cordial on hand to add more flavor. Herbal teas are caffeine-free and often have medicinal benefits, too. Even better, they taste great cold—a requisite when your baby interrupts your tea break!

A blender can become a busy mom's best friend. Experiment with smoothie and soup recipes for a delicious new take on fast food that will help to keep energy levels up throughout the day.

Pin notes or stickers around the house as a reminder to do your pelvic floor exercises. If you are in the car, get used to doing them every time you stop for a red light. You can't overdo these exercises!

As you adjust to life with your new friend, try to rest or sleep when your baby does and find a rhythm for the day together. Never, ever feel guilty about sleeping in the day!

Send a bunch of flowers to your midwife. Could you have done it without her?

It's impossible to "spoil" a new baby with cuddles and kisses. If "well meaning" relatives tell you otherwise, just take a deep breath and ignore them.

The house might be a mess, but so what? Relax and enjoy your new days as a mother. As one short and beautiful bit of verse reminds us: "Cleaning and scrubbing can wait for tomorrow, for babies grow up, I've learned, to my sorrow. So quiet down cobwebs. Dust, go to sleep. I'm rocking my baby, and babies don't keep." Fix this on your refrigerator.

Remember, other people won't "break" your baby, so don't hesitate to hand her over, and never be afraid to ask for help when you need it. Even an hour with your hands free can present an amazingly refreshing break.

Make time for your partner. Although a new baby can absorb every waking moment, there are other people who love you too.

Try carrying your baby in a sling; they love the closeness of your body and you can do most day-to-day activities with ease.

Marvel at your new ability to put the kettle on, brush your hair, and fold the washing with one hand. Celebrate your new skills, and look down at the reason for your newfound dexterity—a baby tucked snugly in the crook of your arm. You may feel like never letting her go!

Love yourself without makeup—your beauty, as a mother, is something that could never fit into a tube or bottle.

> *The moment a child is born, the mother is also born. She never existed before. The woman existed, but the mother, never. A mother is something absolutely new.*
>
> *RAJNEESH*

Look in the mirror and welcome your new self—now a mom—to the world. Celebrate the shape of your body. You've been bigger, and you will be smaller, but for now, just love it the way you are. You may not be aware of it, particularly if you are tired, but new mothers have the most special glow and beauty, and it's all natural.

Taste what your baby tastes and try some breast milk or formula. Feeding a baby is one of the most satisfying jobs on earth.

Cherish the warmth and glow of holding a baby, even long past her bedtime. Enjoy every moment; they grow up too quickly.

*When your milk comes in,
take a moment to giggle at
your perfect Baywatch boobs!*

*If you find you have sore
nipples when breastfeeding,
take a tip from granny and
place macerated cabbage
leaves in your bra to ease
the discomfort.*

After a restless night with your baby, place cotton pads soaked in chamomile tea on your eyelids to soothe tired eyes.

Ask if a partner or friend could mind your baby and book in for a massage. It's a perfect way to nurture your body in the early days, and can either relax or invigorate you, depending upon what you most need!

You and your baby shared a powerful journey through labor. A trip to a cranial osteopath is a gentle way for both of you to realign and help your bodies to settle into your new life. What's more, there's plenty of research showing that colic, frequent crying, and poor sleep habits respond well to this treatment. Give yourself a break!

Keep a selection of news clippings and stories to stick into a scrapbook for your baby, and try to find time to keep it up as she grows. Memories are made of stuff like this, and you can pore over it together when she's a little older.

Keep a radio on in the background when you are at home with your baby so you feel that you always have company. Most new moms don't have much time to read, so you can keep in touch with the outside world without lifting a finger.

Many companies offer diaper laundry services—a good option if you don't want to use disposables, or like the idea of cloth but not the work that this entails!

Use affirmations to boost your self-esteem. These are simple words of positive encouragement that, when spoken aloud, can really help to nurture a sense of calm—or get you back on track when the going is tough. For example: "I am still beautiful"; "Things are getting easier"; "I'm managing better every day"; and "My body has done the most amazing thing I could ever imagine."

Make up your own affirmations for being a mom, and stick them around the house on note cards.

reaching out

As a mom you are part of a "secret," hugely exclusive club, making it so much easier to strike up conversations with other moms you've never met.

Make time in your day to see other adults. It doesn't mean that you love your baby any less, but it can provide invaluable social interaction.

Host a "pot luck" lunch with other new moms. If everyone brings one dish, you all get to eat without the hassle of cooking a big meal.

Start a toy-share scheme
with other parents. Not only
will you make new friends,
but your baby's toys will
seem forever new.

Set up a clothes swap. Some of your
pre-pregnancy clothes may no longer
be "you" (or the right size), and you
may find willing takers for some of
your maternity wear. Not only will
you clear clutter and gain a new
wardrobe, but you'll be helping the
environment by recycling.

If you want to see the latest blockbuster, many local movie theaters hold regular mother-and-baby screenings, where no one minds if there is a bit of background noise. If your local theater doesn't do them, ask them if they'll consider starting.

Join a belly-dancing class. This is one place where having a belly will certainly be celebrated, and you can hone yours to perfection and release a little tension while you are at it.

If the weather is clear, organize a picnic with other new moms.

Get involved in a babysitting circle; leaving your child with another parent is an easy, cheap way to make a little time for yourself, and many other moms will love a little free time of their own, too! If the prospect of watching more than one baby daunts you, consider joining up with a friend to ease the burden.

Hold a buggy race with a few other moms. Line up the buggies in a local park, agree a finishing point, and run. Take it easy if you've just given birth—your body may not match your competitive spirit!

Get into practice for school sports days in the future by arranging an egg and spoon race with other parents. Anything that gets you out and about will not only get those feel-good endorphins flowing, but also help you to regain your pre-pregnancy fitness levels.

Try to see the funny side of being a mom; a big belly laugh burns more calories than you might realize, and when you are about to snap, provides a huge sense of relief.

Now you are out of maternity clothes, go on a shopping spree to find clothes that fit and suit the new you. If you aren't at the weight you'd like to be, find a few inexpensive pieces to mix and match, and some new accessories to tide you over and update your wardrobe in the interim.

Treat yourself to a fabulous
pair of new sunglasses.
You can step outside feeling
super glam, even if baby
kept you awake last night.

*If you ever feel you might have the baby
blues, don't be scared to chat to your doctor
about getting some extra support. Sometimes
just a sympathetic ear and a reassuring
chat can make all the difference. Postnatal
illness is common, and there's no shame in
feeling low. With a little intervention, you'll
soon be back to your old self.*

To keep your spirits high when you are with your baby, learn a new joke every day. She might not understand it, but she'll find your enthusiasm and laughter magical.

Write your own stand-up routine. Some of the less glamorous aspects of being a new mom should give you plenty of material. If nothing else, you'll make yourself, your partner, and probably your baby laugh, and put things into perspective.

Record your baby on video regularly. It's amazing how quickly we forget the little things, and the huge changes that occur in those early weeks and years.

Make a pact with your friends to talk about things that are not baby-related at least some of the time. You may be amazed by how cheering a little adult conversation can be, and how little you really knew about your new friends.

Network! You may not plan to return to work, or you may have plenty of time before you even contemplate the prospect, but contacts will always come in handy and some of the best entrepreneurs are new moms who put their heads together and came up with miracles!

Take over a corner of a café, and nurse your coffee and snacks for a cozy afternoon with friends. Getting out of the house can be a great respite from the daily grind.

Nothing has a better effect upon children than praise.

SIR PHILIP SIDNEY

Spending time with other moms is great, but don't forget to stay in touch with friends who don't have families yet.

To remind yourself that you can still be a mom and feel sexy, sign up for a salsa class. The Latino steps might be just the boost you need to feel good in your body again.

If you feel a new baby is putting a strain on your relationship, get romantic and learn to ballroom dance with your partner. If babysitters are a problem, dim the lights, and dance in your living room.

The soul is healed by being with children.

FYODOR DOSTOYEVSKY

Order a takeout, light some candles, put on some smoochy music, and have a romantic "date" at home with your partner. Even if it seems like hard work at the time, you'll both enjoy being alone together and feeling a little of that old buzz.

Moms need to unwind at the end of the day, too. Don't feel guilty about that glass of wine, which can do wonders to provide instant relaxation. As long as you don't overdo it, your baby will be fine!

Savor the taste of shellfish, soft cheese, and all the other things that you were unable to eat while you were pregnant. If anything seems to give your baby a funny tummy, eat them after a feed, which gives your body plenty of time to clear it out before the next session.

When you feel your normal sexual self again, don't forget the contraception. It is most certainly a myth that you can't get pregnant while breastfeeding!

Turn your kitchen into Vegas! Get together and (learn to) play poker with other moms. No money needs to change hands with Mom's Poker. Be inventive with the chips: breast pads, rusks, or carrots will do. Or how about chits for services—an hour's babysitting, a tray of cookies, a glass of wine upon request. Anything goes!

*Start a "share club" with
other moms and take a
little flutter on stocks and
shares. You'll resharpen
your mind, and might earn
a little money on the side.*

If you used to enjoy quiz shows,
why not follow the formula and start
daytime café quizzes with a group of
mothers. If there's no obvious venue,
have a regular evening, taking turns
at different homes. You'll find some
great quizzes on the internet, and if
everyone brings a bottle of wine or
a plate of snacks, you don't need to
blow your budget.

You can still get to the theater now you are a mom. Look out for outdoor performances in parks during summer months, and even previews and rehearsals for shows by local theater groups. They'll be starting and stopping, so a little noise from your baby won't disrupt too much.

Step into a league of your own and form a five-a-side soccer team with other moms. Not only is soccer fantastic exercise and a great team-building sport, but you'll hold your own when your baby is ready to dribble a ball.

If you're not sure how to meet more women with babies search online for sites such as www.cafemom.com. Look for local mother and baby groups, or hang out in the trendy new "breastfeeding cafés."

Avoid comparing developmental stages with friends' babies; all children develop at their own pace and will do things in their own time.

Instead of thinking about all the things that you haven't done, list all the things that you have achieved. Put being a mom at the top.

" **She never quite leaves her children at home, even when she doesn't take them along.** "

MARGARET CULKIN BANNING

Children have an amazing capacity to be "in the moment"; if motherhood is taking its toll on your energy because you feel there is too much to do, try to do the same. What needs to be done now? Probably not as much as you think.

For a new take on coffee mornings, why not have a sushi morning instead —socialize, and reap the rewards of mineral-rich nori.

Capture baby hands and feet in a clay print—one day you'll be amazed they had such teeny fingers and toes.

Start a book club with other moms, and agree
to choose books that are available on CD
so you can listen while doing other things.
Alternate between a few great kids'
books and adult things you'd
all like to read. It takes the
pressure off trying to find
time to read a whole
book every month.

*Download podcasts of radio
plays or audio drama—these
are often real treasures and a
simple way for you to soak up
culture while you are busy with
your baby.*

There's nothing wrong with being irreverent. Gather with other moms to share funny or lurid labor and pregnancy stories and then let the conversation naturally expand into post-baby life. You'll be laughing before you know it!

When your heart feels ready
to explode with maternal love,
invest in a karaoke machine
and sing your heart out at home.

Collect every song that mentions moms or babies onto a CD: "Baby Love," "Lady Madonna," "I Got You Babe," "She's Having a Baby." Your partner or visitors might not appreciate your choice in music, but remember, this is your secret pleasure.

Have a good old cry. Sometimes motherhood can be overwhelming, and your fluctuating hormones can release a flood of tears at the most amazingly unsentimental things. It's never wrong to cry, and it can provide a huge release from any tension you may be feeling. You don't need to alarm your baby by howling— just sob to your favorite songs, movies, or television commercials, or even the sight of your baby cooing to herself. Then mop yourself down, and have a good laugh.

Looking after yourself is vital now that you're a mom. Start a food co-op! Buying in bulk is a great way to eat well, meet friends, and save dollars.

" To describe my mother would be to write about a hurricane in its perfect power. "

MAYA ANGELOU

A trip to your local farmers' market can feel more rewarding than a supermarket run. Buying directly from friendly faces cuts down air miles, supports local businesses, and helps build a sense of community. What's more, it's probably healthier too.

Share a thought for moms around the world who produce the food you eat, and aim to buy Fair-Trade products wherever possible.

Organic produce usually contains more vitamins and minerals, which are vital for keeping you healthy as a mom. Eat as many as you can afford, and remember that organic produce contains far fewer pesticides and other nasties, which are passed through breastmilk.

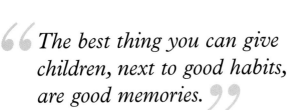

The best thing you can give children, next to good habits, are good memories.

SYDNEY J. HARRIS

Sign up to a local organic box scheme. Fresh produce delivered to your door will give you a bit more time to play or relax with baby, and freshly grown food is always healthier than supermarket alternatives.

Some women face time in prison with babies. Join an organization like womendoingtime.com or writeaprisoner.com and brighten their days by being a pen pal. Think: how would you feel?

If you see changes that you don't like and might affect children (such as closing a local park or amenity) start a buggy blockade. There's a beautiful strength in mothers with babies taking a stand, so never be afraid of making your views known.

Now you are a mom, you've probably noticed how gray the city can look. Brighten up dull areas and become a "Guerrilla Gardener." Plant seeds in random places, and put old bulbs from pots into barren spots.

Our children will be here long after we are gone, and it goes without saying that we have a responsibility to leave them a decent world. Sign petitions for campaigns and causes that will have an impact on their future lives, and take steps at home to be more energy-efficient and environmentally friendly. Sometimes having a baby is all it takes for us to open our eyes to the damage we may be causing.

Moms can be a powerful force in the consumer world—boycott over-packaged baby products and write to manufacturers to explain why.

Anywhere difficult to access with a baby carriage or buggy will also be unavailable to wheelchair users, so complain and make your voice heard.

Plastic bags will outlive your baby, so reuse them whenever you can, and hope hard for a generation who will refuse to use them in the future.

> " Youth fades; love droops; the leaves of friendship fall; a mother's secret hope outlives them all. "

OLIVER WENDELL HOLMES

Babies grow so fast, don't feel that you have to buy everything new. Scour charity stores and local papers for clothes and toys, or visit baby sales at local churches. Keep the cycle going and pass on redundant baby items to other moms or charity stores.

Bag up a bundle of maternity clothes or outgrown baby clothes to sell them on eBay— use the money to buy new ones.

Try to become more aware of the number of chemical-based cleaning products you use, to help protect your baby's environment. Natural alternatives are easy to buy or make. For example, a little essential oil of lemon or tea tree oils added to water make an excellent antibacterial cleanser, and will make your home smell fresh. Blend 10 to 20 drops of eucalyptus oil with 4 cups of water in a spray bottle for a natural disinfectant, or use fresh lemon juice, vinegar, and baking soda to get rid of grease and grime.

It's hard to maintain the juggling act, but try not to ignore letters that might need your attention. Open everything when it arrives, then sort them into trays for urgent or not-so-urgent attention.

If spraying chemical air freshener near a baby feels wrong, fill the house with plants, as they are natural air filters.

Protect the oceans that our children will swim in and replace harsh chemicals with vinegar to clean the toilet.

You're so busy as a mom you don't want to be forever changing light bulbs. Swap normal bulbs for energy-saving ones——they last for years and cut energy bills.

Set up bill payments by direct debit, leaving you free to catch up on sleep or play with your baby without having to worry about final demands. More importantly, perhaps, most direct debit schemes save you a little money.

66 The role of mother is probably the most important career a woman can have. 99

JANET MARY RILEY

If a daily newspaper feels like an extravagant waste because you never get to finish it, start reading your favorite paper online.

The last thing you need is a daily supermarket trip. Cut down on time spent shopping and buy everyday products in the largest sizes available. Consider shopping online or doing mini-shops locally.

One thing that being a mom teaches you is how to prioritize your time; celebrate this and never feel guilty about the things you choose to let go of.

Book in for a first aid course so you won't panic if your baby ever has an accident.

 Motherhood has a very humanizing effect. Everything gets reduced to essentials.

MERYL STREEP

To regain your prepregnancy posture, walk around the house with a book on your head!

Explore the possibilities of yoga, as it can be a great way to relax and get into shape after birth. Yoga also helps to develop your baby's coordination and awareness of her body. It's good for both of you, so why not give it a go? If there are no yoga classes in your area, look for a book and practice at home with baby.

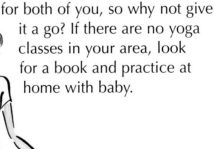

If you don't fancy yoga, buy an exercise DVD and have fun getting fit in the comfort of your living room, at your own pace. Your baby will undoubtedly find your efforts hilarious!

Babies spend a lot of time sky-gazing, so join in! Lie back and relax as you watch clouds vaporize and float across the sky. See what faces, shapes, or animals you can make out in the cloud formations. Teach your baby to find magic in the natural world.

If you feel invincible (and you should) after giving birth, why not try becoming a world record breaker. There's a record for almost everything, from balancing sugar cubes to undoing bra straps. A little distraction therapy never hurt!

Share the fun of going for a group world record with other moms. Even if you don't succeed it's guaranteed to be lots of fun trying.

On a hot summer's day, put your swimsuit on and run under a sprinkler with your baby. It's a great way to cool down and to have fun together.

If you worry about losing pregnancy weight, avoid soda drinks and find a recipe for super-refreshing, homemade lemonade or gather elderflowers to make the sweetest-tasting cordial. Not only are they natural, but they taste great and will make you feel invigorated.

*Find a book that shows just how much
edible food there is in the countryside
and head out for a walk with your
baby to gather new treats. Be careful,
particularly if you are breastfeeding, and
choose the obvious goodies and leave
anything unknown for the birds.*

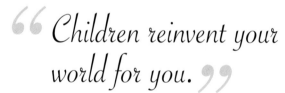

*Children reinvent your
world for you.*

SUSAN SARANDON

For a quick vitamin boost, have you ever thought about freezing fruit-juice into popsicle molds? Smoothies, with or without yogurt, can be frozen in the same way for an instant, healthy treat.

You do so, so much as a mother, so accept offers of help with grace and allow others to do things for you. If you find yourself with friends who are embarrassed to offer their help, then make a timetable and get everyone to jot down when they can help and what they are prepared to do. If everyone joins in, there will be plenty on offer!

Consider a skill-swapping session. Many new moms are keen to help others, but are more confident about using their own skills. So why not arrange to babysit for someone who can do your accounts, or cook a meal for someone who can walk your dog on rainy mornings. Get the yoga instructor to give you a group session, and you can repay her with homemade meals or babysitting when she needs it.

" A little girl, asked where her home was, replied, "where mother is. "

KEITH L. BROOKS

If you catch the time to cook a meal while your baby is sleeping, double or triple up the ingredients and freeze a few meals for another day.

Sharing a bath with a baby is such good fun and splashing can help little ones to become aware of their hands.

Take a moment to see your house from a baby's point of view. Lie on the floor, tummy down, or gaze at the ceiling—if the panorama is dull, liven it up with bright pictures and objects.

" *There is nothing more thrilling in this world, I think, than having a child that is yours, and yet is mysteriously a stranger.* "

AGATHA CHRISTIE

Start thinking about safety. It isn't long before babies begin to roll and then crawl. In your baby's-eye view of things, what do you see that could present a potential hazard?

66 Before you were conceived I wanted you. Before you were born I loved you. Before you were here an hour I would die for you. This is the miracle of life. 99

MAUREEN HAWKINS

Small babies have no concept of space and time——this is one of the reasons why they love to play peek-a-boo. Engage as much as you can. This will make them laugh for more years than you can imagine!

Gentle tickling games encourage babies to laugh. Not only is it one of the most beautiful sounds imaginable, but you'll be helping to develop their speech, too.

Why splash out on expensive baby toys? Look around the house for (safe) objects that can become playthings. Pots, pans, wooden spoons, measuring jugs, pins, and even clothes are great toys, as long as they are clean.

" To show a child what once delighted you, to find the child's delight added to your own, this is happiness. "

J.B. PRIESTLEY

Go out for a walk and gather natural objects to make a mobile: dried leaves, pine cones, pebbles, dried flowers, and berries look beautiful when they are hung. Glue them together with nontoxic adhesives, or hang them individually to create a gorgeous, natural display.

Make an effort to befriend moms with disabled children. Remember the extra challenges they may face on top of adjusting to motherhood.

Introduce your child to friends and family who live far away. Use their photos in a mobile and hang it in a place where your baby spends a lot of time. Sometimes just telling stories about people in a photo album will make absent friends and family part of daily life.

Place a photo of yourself next to your baby's crib or cot, so it's the first thing they see when they wake up.

Find a baby picture of yourself and look for any facial resemblances that you share with your child—how intriguing it is to wonder what they might look like when they are your age.

Who else can you see when you gaze at your baby? Your partner? Your mother? Yourself? It's fascinating to observe familial similarities. And it's not just features; expressions are also inherited. You may find that your baby scowls in just the same way as your father, or holds his hands just like your grandfather.

Family faces are magic mirrors. Looking at people who belong to us, we see the past, present, and future.

GAIL LUMET BUCKLEY

getting

cozy

Now that you're a Mom, try baking a pie and take a moment to tell yourself that you are absolutely perfect. If it doesn't work—hey, you tried!

Invent a new recipe and name it after your baby. This may take several attempts!

Make your favorite cake from childhood and don't feel any guilt about eating it all in one go (with friends or without).

On a clear night, wrap yourself and baby up warm and step outside to watch the stars.

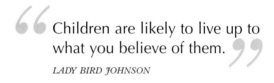

" Children are likely to live up to what you believe of them. **"**

LADY BIRD JOHNSON

The next time you see a shooting star, make a wish for your child.

Now you are a mom you'll probably take greater pleasure in simple, but magic, moments. Find a beautiful place to watch the sun setting. Watch a bird lining her nest, a squirrel collecting nuts, the dew collected on your garden leaves, the frost on the windows, the raindrops. Stopping to stare is not only life-affirming, but also reminds you of what your baby will be seeing for the very first time.

Take an enchanted early morning walk in a dew-filled garden. There are some advantages to getting up early with a baby!

Don't curse if baby wakes you before dawn; meet others who are awake at that time too and visit a flower market.

Learn to predict the weather by reading the clouds. It's a novel way to pass time and you will (hopefully) avoid ever getting caught out in the rain with your baby.

Some things seem magical, no matter how old you are. Head out for a night walk to see if you can find fireflies dancing.

Moms need cuddles, too! A big hug increases levels of the feel-good hormone serotonin in your brain. Never be afraid to ask for hugs of your own, and if you are feeling deprived, snuggle up with your baby and feel her tiny arms enclose you.

Show your baby the beauty and majesty of a thunderstorm. If you find them alarming, learn to love them so that your baby will, too. Children pick up more than you may think from their primary carers.

Take a walk in the country with your baby and gather natural treasures for a nature table. It's a great way to recapture elementary school memories, and to let your child explore the multitude of textures, shapes, and smells that make up the natural world.

Stand in the rain and teach your baby to catch raindrops on her tongue. Snowflakes are even better.

On the days when being a mom seems a little overwhelming, take a trip to the nearest beach or river. Throwing pebbles into water is a great way to release tension. Can you skip stones? Your baby will be intrigued and impressed by your skill.

Surrounding yourself with gorgeous smells is one way to boost your spirits when motherhood seems to keep you forever busy. Essential oils are obvious ones, but why not get in some pots of fresh herbs, some wild flowers from the woods or local fields, or even half a lemon with a handful of cilantro left open to excite your senses.

Send a message in a bottle out to sea and make a wish that another mom will find it. If your message is answered, make sure you respond as well.

Put a birdfeeder in the garden and see how many birds you can name to your baby as they come to feed. If in doubt, borrow a bird book from the library and show the pictures to your new best friend.

Some days fly past and some seem to go on forever when you are a mom. When was the last time you used a dandelion clock to tell the time? Legend has it that the number of breaths it takes to blow off all the seeds of a dandelion globe that has gone to seed, is the hour number. Time, anyone?

Gather seasonal berries and fruit to freeze or preserve, so you and your child can enjoy fruit all year round that isn't flown across the world. Local produce is healthier because it doesn't sit in the back of a truck or on a supermarket shelf. The faster you preserve or freeze it, the better.

Make a "sun catcher" with glass paints, or find a beautiful prism or crystal to dangle in a window for your baby to see. She'll be attracted by the light and will marvel in the colors.

See how many different constellations you can learn and spot in the sky, and name them to your baby as you learn to recognize them. There's no reason why you can't identify a special group of stars and name a new constellation in honor of your child. Point it out across the years, and make her feel special.

Sheepskin is great for babies, but have you ever considered asking a farmer to make one rather than buying one in a shop?

Little ones love bright colors so, even if you aren't a natural artist, try painting bright bold patterns or swirls with poster paints on her walls or even windows.

What will your baby look like when she is five, or even ten? Have some fun and make a portrait of what you imagine her to look like. Tuck it away and compare at the appropriate time!

Paint a portrait of mother and baby. It's a theme that winds through art across the centuries, and it's beautiful. Don't worry about perfection or even accuracy. Be expressive and unleash the artist in you!

Frame a lock or curl of your child's baby hair, or tuck it away in your memory box. Take a snip every year or so. Our children's hair may change color many times as they head towards adulthood, and it's lovely to see that transformation in concrete terms.

Start collecting board games for a games cabinet, and try to remember the rules for some of your old favorites.

It's all too easy to turn on the TV when your child goes to sleep. Switch it off and read a book instead. Or sleep yourself.

Relive your own childhood. Feel like a child again and kick autumn leaves high in the air or splash in big puddles. Collect leaves and conkers, or make huts from garden furniture. What do you remember from your own childhood? If it formed the stuff of memories, it's worth doing again with your little one.

You will be your child's first teacher. Study a dictionary to find a new word every day and remember what it feels like to learn. Use the word when you talk to your children. There's plenty of research suggesting that children who hear huge vocabularies develop them. Give him a head start!

Fill your garden with nightlights, and take an enchanted evening walk with your baby.

One day your baby will be fascinated by photos of you as a child, so take the time to organize loose pictures into albums. Or make a collage from pictures of you at each age group, so he can contrast and compare as he grows ever bigger.

Babies grow so fast; in just a short time you'll be amazed how tiny they were. Be sure to capture the changes with lots of photos. When you have your final prints, write the date and subject on the back. In a few years' time you won't believe how much you have forgotten.

Play with new techniques for gorgeous baby pictures: experiment with black-and-white images, take shots in unusual settings, and have fun with the self-timer button on your camera to make sure photos include you as well as baby.

Indulge! Book a session in a photography studio to have a professional portrait taken of you and your baby.

Friends and family who live far away will cherish pictures as your baby grows. You can set up a private photo gallery on many internet-based photo-sharing sites. It's a lot cheaper than mailing updates.

Phone up a radio station and dedicate a song to yourself for being such a great mom.

Why not set up regular payments into a savings account for your child —even a little a month will set up a useful nest egg for the future.

Keep a video diary of your days as a mom—these early days will pass faster than you think.

Writing is a brilliant way to share the joy and happy memories motherhood brings, and is also a safe way to express any worries or pent-up feelings you might have as a mom. Why not keep a journal? For one thing, it will remind you of all those "firsts" and milestones that are so easily forgotten as time passes.

Start an online blog to record your thoughts and feelings as a new mother, and invite comments from other moms. There is nothing like sharing the joys and pitfalls of parenting with others who understand.

Mothers have written many beautiful poems about children. If you find one that resonates with your feelings, copy it out and frame it.

Write a poem for your baby,
to see if you can encapsulate
the love you feel in words.

Enjoy the humor of being a mom and write a limerick about your child: "There was a young baby called …" It won't be long before your baby can recite it back to you!

"Just keep a spring in your heart and…ask yourself, "Where's my sense of humor?"

MAE WEST

Being a mom doesn't mean you can't look glamorous. Even if you're staying in for the evening, get dressed up and put on a little makeup—if only for your own pleasure!

Having a baby can provide you with a greater awareness of the chemicals in many cosmetics, personal hygiene and baby products. Simple kitchen ingredients can provide a wealth of cheap, natural alternatives. For example, good-quality olive oil can make an excellent moisturizer for mother and baby and can help to ease the itching of cradle cap, and soothe diaper rash. A mashed avocado makes a healthy, vitamin-E packed facial mask.

For a little rejuvenating "me" time after a hectic day with a baby, add a few drops of geranium oil to warm water, soak a face cloth in the solution, place it over your face for ten minutes, and relax.

If you worry that your new sleep patterns are taking their toll on your complexion, indulge in a home facial to cleanse, tone, and nourish.

Your lustrous pregnancy locks do, sadly, thin after birth, but don't despair! Take time to get a great new haircut or color, and take a moment to celebrate your body returning to its former glory!

Asking someone to read a story aloud to you while you are tucked up in bed will remind you why children love this so much.

Remember that it's never too early to read to your baby—she'll love the sound of your voice, even if you are only reading your own books aloud!

If you are too sleepy to take much in from a book, or you want to read while feeding why not listen to an audiobook instead?

Did your own mom or grandmother make your clothes? Have some fun yourself! Dust off that sewing machine and buy a pattern. Polishing your skills will be a bonus when it comes time to make costumes for Hallowe'en or the school play. You may even be inspired to make some soft furnishings to decorate your baby's room.

If you find that looking after a baby makes you forgetful, invest in a whiteboard and pin it up in the kitchen where you'll be reminded constantly of what's coming up.

Your baby loves the sound of your voice, and even early on learns speech patterns and intonation. So keep up the chatter—talk about anything and everything. She doesn't need to understand what you are saying to benefit and enjoy your company.

Ask yourself why the sky is blue, and what rainbows are made of, in preparation for the many questions that will be coming your way in just a few years.

The word "infant" means "not able to speak," but that doesn't mean that you don't understand their signs and signals. Hold her and chat to her as often as you can—you'll be amazed by the feedback you get! And you'll soon learn to recognize when she's not happy, and wants something else.

If time is tight, turn your kitchen into a salon and book a visit from a mobile hairdresser. Or get a group of girls round and give each other a pedicure. A little pampering can do wonders for your morale now that you're a mom.

Moms don't get sick pay or days off, so keep your immune system strong and healthy with plenty of vitamin C. Try taking the herb Echinacea at the first signs of illness. Natural remedies are much safer for baby if you are breastfeeding, and there are loads to choose from! A steam inhalation with a couple of drops of eucalyptus oil can help to clear congestion, and lavender oil dabbed neat on your temples, will ease a headache.

Grow an aloe vera plant. The gel from their leaves is an excellent addition to any natural first-aid kit, and can safely treat your baby's burns, bites, or stings.

Take your baby on a "date." Dress up and have lunch in a restaurant that you've always wanted to go to.

Imagine what your baby's voice will sound like when she does start talking.

It's all too easy to lavish time and attention on a baby and forget yourself; try to eat when baby eats, even if it's only a snack. Your baby will learn to enjoy food by watching you, and soon be eager to feed herself.

Make a special compilation CD filled with songs that hit the charts in the month of your baby's birth. Or simply choose songs that mean something to you, and put them away for your baby to enjoy in the future. Make a few "sleeve notes" to explain why these songs are meaningful.

It's easy to visit art galleries and museums with your baby in a sling, and they are usually quiet enough to let her nap in peace. Enjoy a little culture while you've got the time and a willing partner!

Most babies understand simple gestures, so invent your own sign language. This can help to avoid frustration when they are learning to talk.

a new you

You've grown a baby, so try growing flowers. Plant your child's name in flowers, and watch it bloom in the spring.

Plant vegetables, ready to make the freshest, tastiest purees to tempt your baby when she's a little older.

Even without a garden you and your baby can still enjoy fresh food—sow seeds in containers and window boxes.

Laughter lifts the spirits like nothing else, so organize a babysitter and go to a comedy club. Or sit down to watch a funny movie with your baby. She'll find your giggles infectious!

A box of tissues, chocolate, and a good "weepy" movie might be the perfect way to indulge yourself on a rainy day when baby is sleeping. All "rules" about daytime TV can go out the window in those early days. You need all the indulgence you can get!

Rooiboos tea can help busy moms unwind; it gives you all the cozy comforts of a cup of tea but is high in antioxidants and is also caffeine-free.

A simple way for a busy mom to start the day on a high note is to stand on your head just after getting up.

Positive thoughts can work wonders when the daily grind gets you down. Remember that things might take a little longer, but you are just as capable as you ever were. Try to remove the words "can't," "don't," and "won't" from your vocabulary.

Inspirational books can help you keep a sense of yourself when you are overwhelmed by motherhood. Find an audio version, and listen to it regularly to keep your spirits high, and to help you find the positive in the everyday.

While mothering is always inspiring, it can often be challenging. Read an autobiography by someone who has overcome even bigger obstacles, to help shift your perspective.

Don't start thinking about work before you have to. You never get this precious time back. If the idea is already starting to irk, investigate the possibility of job sharing, going part-time, or working from home. Or, if it's possible, take off a little more time to be with your new friend.

If you've always dreamed of running your own business, harness the extra strength you've found in motherhood as a platform to succeed.

Many women find that motherhood changes their perspective, and their dreams and visions alter. Remember that it's never too late to change direction. Why not use some of the many skills you've learned as a mom or head back to college?

Children are born assuming that mom and dad know everything! Keep an encyclopedia in the bathroom to expand your repertoire of random facts.

When you stop breastfeeding treat yourself to some sexy and slinky new underwear. So what if your tummy still looks a bit wobbly after giving birth? Buy a pair of "magic" panties and you can wear anything you want to.

You are beautiful as a mom, but if you feel self-conscious about your figure shift the focus of attention—wear a backless dress for a special night out.

Sign up for an evening class and gain new skills in a hobby or subject you've always wanted to learn more about. Or find a local college and pop your baby in the nursery for a few hours while you get a little extra stimulation.

There can be no better time than early motherhood to face up to a few phobias. Aim to overcome the one thing that has always scared you, not only to prevent your baby from absorbing and developing your own fears, but also to have a clearer idea of the constant challenges your baby faces in the big, wide world.

Every mom has down days, but gritting your teeth and "faking" a smile can not only make you feel happier, but you'll get some of the real thing back, which will undoubtedly lift your spirits.

There is only one pretty child in the world, and every mother has it.

CHINESE PROVERB

Life as a mother means learning to juggle your life. Turn it around and learn to juggle like a clown.

Share the joy of motherhood and perform a random act of kindness. The "helpers' high" experienced from doing a good deed releases endorphins that make you feel even better.

Some moms love the experience of childbirth so much that they train as midwives once their babies are older—this might be a new avenue for you to explore. Or maybe you'd just like to help other mothers-to-be prepare for the birth? Is there an opening at your local childbirth group for a helper?

If the thought of leaving your baby to return to work is too daunting, consider becoming a childminder yourself—or working at home with a few hours of help when baby isn't sleeping.

If childcare arrangements have to be made, start early so that you get exactly what you want for your special baby. Do your homework and follow your instincts. Ask to spend a whole morning at a nursery rather than making a brief visit. It will help you to understand your baby's new environment, and reassure you that it is just right for him.

If you miss clubbing now that you have a baby, learn to DJ with your favorite records in the comfort of your own home. Your growing baby will undoubtedly enjoy the music, and if you dance along, you will be the source of much entertainment!

One outrageous way to get your body back in shape after birth is to sign up for pole-dancing classes, and for the less adventurous, the hula-hoop will shed pounds.

Resist the temptation to have a cigarette again if you were a smoker before getting pregnant. It only takes one to become an addict.

Try not to swear in front of your child; it's a good habit to get into before they start to copy your words. Think of some inventive and harmless expletives instead.

> Life is the first gift, love is the second, and understanding the third.

MARGE PIERCY

Sing with other moms—start a local choir or chamber group, or just get together to sing folk songs or old favorites. There is such beauty in women singing together, and babies will be enchanted by the sound. Chants and songs from around the world are some of the easiest melodies to sing in perfect harmony and express the joy of motherhood.

Join a samba band; there's nothing like banging your own drum now that you are a mom. And there can, surely, be no other way to release a little frustration than to drum it out!

If you can give birth, you can do anything. While you are at home with your baby, why not learn to play an instrument? Or just bang away on a piano or keyboard to your heart's content. Babies love music, and you may well inspire him to follow suit!

If your head feels cluttered while you are at home with your baby, reorganize the furniture to see if this helps nurture a sense of calm. Or do a little DIY feng shui—clearing the clutter and letting the energy flow can give you a new lease of life.

Research shows that talking to others increases feelings of happiness and relaxation. So gather with other moms and chatter for as long as you want to, with the added knowledge that you are doing each other good.

Becoming a mother moves us closer to believing that nothing is impossible, and that the world is full of new possibilities. Harness this feeling and learn to walk on fire—with professional guidance, it really can be done. Or take your biggest dream and double it.

For an easy way to exercise, try buggy-jogging. Get behind your buggy and run! Ask other moms to join in for a little company—and healthy competition!

Even though you might feel tired, physical activity can help you to feel reenergized. Wrap up baby and take a brisk walk, or just meander in the park for a few hours to get your blood going.

Leave the car at home and take your baby out in a buggy or sling—they'll see and hear more of their world than they ever will through a car window.

❝ Making the decision to have a child— it's momentous. It is to decide forever to have your heart go walking around outside your body. ❞

ELIZABETH STONE

Take advantage of nursery facilities to get a little exercise, take a swim, or just wallow in a steam bath for an hour or so. Your baby will enjoy the new sights and sounds of a busy childcare facility, and you'll get a much-needed break.

If you can't squeeze into your favourite prepregnancy jeans yet, find a picture of the pregnant you and marvel at how much bigger you were. Things can only get better!

Cut out pictures of a celebrity mom that you admire, who isn't a size zero, and emulate her style.

Moms can still be glamorous. If you want to wear heels but worry about pushing a buggy in stilettos, invest in a pair of wedges.

You'll find you have a fierce new protective instinct, and that you'd fight tooth and nail for your little one. If you ever feel a little vulnerable, why not take a self-defense class to equip yourself for any situation?

Gaze in the mirror and take pleasure in noticing how toned your arms are becoming, just from carrying a baby.

Now you're a mom you can roller skate, and keep your dignity intact—get ready to teach baby.

Buy a trampoline. They are great for body-toning and aerobic exercise, and your baby can enjoy it soon.

Go swimming in a baby pool and simply enjoy being eye-to-eye in the water together. If you are having a fractious day, head straight down to the pool. Warm water and gentle splashing will calm even the grumpiest little one.

If you relish the thought of having a long swim alone, try a late-night session, as this might be an easier time to arrange childcare.

Laugh, as you realize that you have a genuine reason to visit toyshops again. What was your favorite toy as a child? Can you still get it?

Read up on common childhood ailments, so you feel fully prepared when you need to care for a sick baby.

To keep your skin baby-soft, infuse a handful of chamomile flowers in a jar of olive oil. It's safe, sweet-smelling, relaxing, and mild enough for baby and you. Use it within a month.

Explore the possibilities of complementary therapies as a gentle way to nurture baby and you; many moms don't like the idea of invasive treatments for their little ones, and even for themselves while breastfeeding. It's amazing how many common ailments can be dealt with by trained practitioners. Homoeopathy, flower essences, and aromatherapy seem to be particularly good for mother and baby.

We tend to dream more when sleep is interrupted. Keep a dream diary and look up their meanings.

Learn to knit—it's a great way to create really special baby clothes and gives you a practical reason to sit down and relax.

Embroider your child's name into a
sampler, frame it, and hang it in her
bedroom. Even if the stitches are
wobbly it will always be special.

"There are two lasting bequests
we can give our children. One
is roots. The other is wings."

HODDING CARTER, JR.

To liven up boring all-in-ones without using harsh chemicals, experiment with natural dyes. Many, such as turmeric, beet, and red cabbage, can be found in your pantry!

Knit your baby a special blanket and add a wish with each color of wool you use.

Bring new life to outgrown clothes and make a rag doll. It's the sort of toy that your child will cherish for years (boys too!).

Stitch memories of these early days with your baby into a patchwork quilt. Some moms like to use bits of fabric from favorite baby blankets and articles of clothing, so that each panel holds a "memory."

Babies have a huge repertoire of expressions. Have fun mimicking them, as they will often find this hilarious. Hold up a mirror so he can see himself and puzzle at the funny baby reflection.

Your home should be a representation of the new you. Get rid of anything that no longer seems to reflect the changes you feel, and make some room in your house and heart for all the new possibilities that lie ahead.

How many nursery rhymes or songs from your own childhood can you remember now that you want to sing them to your child? Invest in a good book or CD and relearn them. Nursery songs are a great way to encourage a child's vocabulary and memory, and also to inspire a love of music.

Make some noise with a "baby band." Pull out pots and pans from the kitchen cupboards and bash away with wooden spoons!

Moms might have mountains of washing, but placing a washing line above head-height turns drying clothes into a posture-improving exercise rather than just a chore.

If baby clothes turn gray in the wash, tie-dye them for a new lease of life.

You are perfect just as you are, so avoid the temptation to compare your achievements with anyone else's. The same goes for baby. All little ones develop at different paces, and your baby will be perfect just the way she is.

If the thought of a night on the town no longer appeals now that you are a mom, make your nights in indulgent—run a hot, scented bubble bath, light a few candles, pour a glass of wine, and relax.

Any mother could perform the jobs of several air-traffic controllers with ease.

LISA ALTHER

celebrations

Make a time capsule.
Gather words, pictures,
and mementos that reflect
your baby's birth and
early likes and dislikes,
and enclose them in a
water-tight box or jar.
Bury it in a special place.

Try to learn more about your
family and its history—one day
your baby will love to know
where she came from.

See how far back you can trace
your maternal family tree, with the
joy of knowing that you have now
added another branch to it.

You might view your
parents in a new light
now that you're a mom.
Use your new knowledge
to forge a stronger bond
with them, and be aware
that they will see you
differently now too.

Ask your parents to share memories of you as a baby, and take the opportunity to look through old childhood photos. Is your baby like you in more ways than one?

Seize motherhood as a powerful opportunity to reflect on your own childhood; record your thoughts and memories.

Make a list of the things that provide you with the most vivid memories, and try to recreate them for your own baby. Simple songs, days out, even a favorite mobile, can stick in our minds for decades. Give your child something special to remember as well.

If your mom finds it difficult to adjust to her new role, charm her with an entry in a "Glamorous Granny" competition.

All parents make mistakes and you will, too, so don't be too hard on your own parents. Instead, embrace new ways of doing things and combine them with some of the things you know your own mom got right.

Becoming a mom can bring a new perspective to your parents' actions. A very honest letter can help you to share new understandings or release old issues, even if you never actually send it.

Know that babies have a way of opening our hearts to love and forgiveness, so try to let go of old hurts and anger with parents, siblings, or past relationships. You'll find a real sense of freedom as negative feelings shift away.

Reward yourself for being a great mom with a huge bouquet of flowers. There's plenty of research suggesting that flowers can raise spirits and increase your sense of happiness.

It's good for moms to nurture their inner child, and laughter is the perfect way to do this. So, celebrate April Fools' Day with the sheer joy of a cheeky child and play some practical jokes. Humor is contagious!

You'll never forget your first Mother's Day. Ask someone to take a photo of you, your baby, and even your own mom, and capture the day forever.

Do something extra special for your mom on Mother's Day to acknowledge that she is readjusting to a new role, too, and to celebrate the fact that you now understand what it's like to be a parent.

Memories of special days with your new baby can be kept forever. Gather mementoes of your adventures together in a scrapbook and label them. As he gets older, she can add her own comments, or at least help with the cutting and pasting!

Invent a story with your baby as the central character and type it up. When he's old enough, you can ask him to illustrate it for you.

Copy your story into a special notebook and add pictures: photos, postcards, or your drawings. Your child will love it when she is older.

Homemade gifts give so much pleasure. Try making soap and create a label inspired by your child's name. Or put her fledgling stirring skills to the test and create a culinary masterpiece with her help.

Candles are used in countless celebrations and, since you will have so many more reasons to celebrate now that you're a mom, why not learn how to make your own? Adorn them with crystals and scent them with essential oils for a truly magical experience.

Even if you are not religious, holding a naming ceremony for your baby is a wonderful way to welcome her to the world.

Buy a copy of Cinderella for a special female friend and ask her if she will be your child's fairy godmother.

Hold a party for close friends who've been a big help to you as a new mom.

If you get an invitation to a "childfree" wedding, suggest sharing the cost of a nanny with other parents—it might be easier than turning down the invite or making elaborate childcare arrangements.

Is your baby a Leo or a Libran? Learning about astrology can give you new insights into your baby's temperament.

Discover enough about astrology to work out your baby's birth chart. You don't have to believe it all, but it can be fascinating to see how her life might pan out. Birth charts make great presents for other friends with children, too.

Each month is associated with a flower—find the flower that represents the month of your baby's birth and your own, and press and frame them together.

Plant a "family garden," choosing the flowers that represent each member of your family's birthdates.

Buy a pretty piece of jewelery with your baby's birthstone to offer as a "naming" gift, or just to celebrate her birth.

Our ancestors marked the year according to the phases of the moon (the lunar cycle), and believed that each cycle is linked to a tree. Choose the tree that represents the moon at your child's birth (you can find this in a Celtic tree calendar, if you are stuck), and plant one to honor your child's birth.

As you celebrate your child's first birthday, stop for a moment and think of other moms who are also cherishing this day.

A first birthday is a milestone to celebrate, but you might also feel surprisingly emotional. Try not to fight these bittersweet emotions and take a moment in the day for reflection.

Ask your mom for the recipe of your favorite childhood cake.

Celebrate your day of giving birth and buy yourself a pair of glam shoes or a handbag.

Eggs are given at Easter because they are a symbol of life and rebirth. You've brought new life into the world, so buy yourself a giant Easter egg to celebrate.

Motherhood is a daily celebration, which is, perhaps, why festivals all around the world invite us to connect with our inner child. Explore those that are unfamiliar, such as Holi, the Indian Festival of Color, when friends are splashed with brightly colored water.

Small children love the glow of candlelight, so carve a pumpkin for Hallowe'en and share the magic flicker of the lantern with the lights turned off.

Indulge in childhood memories and toast marshmallows over a fire.

Celebrate Divali, the Indian festival of light, in October or November. Light candle lanterns in the garden —it's never too early for your child to learn about other faiths.

Your first Christmas as a mom creates the opportunity to repeat the traditions and rituals that you had as a child. Look through pictures to try to rekindle your memories and then recreate them for your baby.

Make Christmas cards for close family and friends using a photo of your baby.

Your first Christmas with baby will be special, so find some beautiful tree ornaments or decorations that will always remind you of this time. Some moms like to buy each child a special ornament every Christmas—something that reflects their personality or interests, perhaps—with the day inscribed or written on the back. In just a few years, you'll have a tree full of special memories.

Wrap up warm and go out to see the Christmas lights together; small babies are fascinated by the twinkle and sparkle.

Did you have a special Christmas stocking when you were little? Ask your parents if they still have it, so you can pass it on.

Nothing makes you giggle
quite like the first time you get
to "be" Father Christmas and
fill your little one's stocking.
Enjoy the moment!

*Start some new family traditions
now that you're a mom—perhaps
Father Christmas prefers to be left
a glass of wine rather than milk!*

The world seems very big when you are very small. Remember this when you talk to children, and bend down so that you can talk to them face to face.

When it's rainy outside but you feel full of joy inside, put on your favorite music, hold your baby close and just dance.

Instill a love of nature in your baby, by getting out into the natural world every day, rain or shine. Take pleasure in snowflakes, splashing in puddles, collecting leaves, and stopping to admire beautiful flowers.

66 *The best thing you can give children, next to good habits, are good memories.* 99

SYDNEY J. HARRIS

further shores
and faraway
places

Visit elderly relatives—their tips and baby stories can be a treasure trove of wisdom and ideas.

There is often a magical bond between the very old and the very young—watching this interaction between generations can be a moving experience.

If you are an only child, or the first sibling to have a baby, take a moment to honor the fact that you have started a new generation of your family.

Know when to listen and when to disregard the "good advice" that people may send your way. The best moms blend instinct with common sense.

Introduce your hometown to your baby and pretend to be a tourist for the day.

Rediscover your sense of adventure. Feel the wind in your hair and take a trip on an open-top bus. Or ride a train to the end of the line, just to see where it takes you.

Hold a seashell to your baby's ear so she can hear the sound of the sea.

Take your baby for a trip to your old elementary school if they have a concert or summer fête. Wonder at how small everything looks, and how your own baby sees the world.

Find out where your parents lived when you were an infant and visit your first house.

Each place that you visit as a mom will seem forever new if you learn to view your surroundings with the wonder of a child.

Get your baby's first passport as early as you can. You never know when the urge to take off might strike you.

Have fun in a photo booth as you take your child's first passport picture.

If you can't face the thought of negotiating a buggy and a suitcase, try using a backpack.

For magical vacations that your child will always remember, invest in a campervan and go "on the road" as a family.

If the last thing you want to do is travel with a baby, cruise the world from an armchair and read inspirational travel stories.

Days out can be cheap and rewarding. Borrow, hire, or buy a bike with a child's seat and peddle out for the day on an adventure of your choosing.

Enjoy the freedom of traveling with a young baby. She won't wander off or get lost! And you won't have to worry about what she can eat or drink while she's still breastfeeding.

Make the most of being able to travel without the constraints of school vacations.

Maternity leave can be a great time to take minibreaks—why not head out with another mom and her baby for a midweek break. Kids go free when they sit on your knee, so travel while it's cheap.

House swapping with a foreign family can be a great way of taking a vacation complete with all home comforts.

If you're not yet confident about baring all in a bikini after becoming a mom, splash out on a slinky swimsuit and sarong for beach vacations.

When was the last time you saw baboons, elephants, or giraffes? Plan a trip to a safari park, petting farm, or local zoo. Small children are eternally fascinated by animals, and you'll be teaching them a little more about the world around them.

Take a trip to a city farm to remind you of all the farmyard noises—you may be surprised to learn that these are often your baby's first "words."

If you never got the chance to go to Disney World as a child, book up and go with your baby.

Go to a church and light a candle for any moms and babies who might be ill.

Now's your chance to jump into a ball pool! Most towns have a soft-play center, and having a baby means that you get to go in, too.

Walk barefoot in the sand with a newly toddling baby.

Find a stick and write your child's name in six-foot letters on a sandy beach.

The mother's heart is the child's school-room.

HENRY WARD BEECHER

Go beachcombing and use the treasures you find to make a mobile or a picture frame for your child's room.

Capture the joy of your childhood and chase waves as they roll onto the seashore.

Revisit the places you remember having the happiest vacation when you were a child.

Getting together with a group of parents to invest in a time-share, opens up many new possibilities for family vacation.

If you haven't climbed a tree since you were a child, give it a go to recall how much fun it can be. Lift your baby up to touch the branches.

Very few travel agents offer discounts for one adult and child sharing a room. Get vocal and put pressure on them to offer free kids' places for single parents.

If you're a single mom who desperately needs a vacation, explore renting a house with other moms in a similar position.

*Sit in a park on a sunny
day and crown yourself
a fairy-mom with a
daisy chain.*

*Keep old bread for feeding ducks. It's
one of the simplest pleasures to share
with a baby, and it is sure to both
evoke memories of your childhood
and delight your own baby.*

If you don't have the energy to look after a pet, why not adopt an endangered animal in the wild? You'll be doing something positive for your child's future world, and you can use the experience to teach her a little about animals around the world.

To experience a natural force that is nearly as powerful as giving birth, make a trip to see the next solar eclipse.

On a warm summer's night let the moon caress your cares away. Walk naked in the garden with your baby and try moon-bathing.

Now you're a mom, you have a new perspective on what true beauty is. If hotels and beaches seem boring, plan a vacation to see the aurora borealis (northern lights) or take a sailing trip and breathe in the beauty of wind and waves.

Use a backpack to carry older babies. It will create the freedom to go for walks together: to the countryside, seaside and beyond....

Go to a carnival and win a cuddly toy for your child.

Get a friend or partner to hold your baby while you take a ride on the biggest rollercoaster you can find. Let her see your excitement!

Marvel at your child's face as you share her first experience on a carousel.

Find a "secret" place behind a chair or under a blanket for telling magical stories and building a sense of adventure with your baby.

Use time at home to learn a new language. If you listen to lessons together, your baby will absorb new information, too. Make some flashcards as prompts—you can use them in years to come to teach your baby yourself.

Name things aloud for your baby in English and the language you are learning. Not only will it help to cement it in your memory, but she'll be bilingual before you know it.

Live out fairy tales with your baby—visit castles, forests, and palaces, and make up stories as you go.

Discover the stairs together, shuffling up and down the steps with your child. You may not even need a stairgate if she gets the hang of it with mom at her side.

You're a wonder as a mother, so plan a trip to at least one of the Seven Wonders of the World.

If you live far away from the sea, put a sand-box in your garden, so you and you child can pretend you are at the seaside. Build sandcastles and get the garden hose out to create some waves.

What smells evoke your childhood? It might be fun to spend a day seeking them out. Play dough, crayons, gingerbread, and even a summer garden might bring memories flooding back and create new ones for your baby.

Before you became a mom, you would have never imagined the intensity of love you feel for your child—and that it would grow as quickly as they do. Climb to the top of the mountain and shout with joy to express this love.

Write your very own list of things you'd like to do now that you're...a Mom.

adventures
beyond
baby years

Seek out friends with older children. Chatting and playing with them will give you a great sense of all the things you have to look forward to.

Learning how to be a playmate might take time. Enjoy a day being silly—let go, get messy, and get lost in your child's laughter.

Bring your house to life! Play with your child and pretend that the stairs are a mountain, the sofa is a boat, and the table is a castle.

Join a library and see if you can find the books that you loved as a child, then share the pleasure of your memories as you read them together.

Encourage your child to help plant seeds in the garden to ensure your family will enjoy seasonal, organic fruit in years to come.

Gather leaves and flowers that you don't recognize, and look them up with an older child.

Plant bulbs in the garden and every year that they bloom think about how your child will have grown during the past year.

Think back to the things you really wanted to do as a child but never quite managed. Now's the time to reclaim your childhood and take your child down memory lane.

Tip a pile of toys on the floor and let your child lead the play!

Small children create the perfect opportunity to do things you haven't experienced for years: chase bubbles around the garden, splash in a fountain, roll down a hill, or take a jump on a bouncy castle.

Enjoy playing the board games you loved as a child. Arrange fun forfeits for first and second, to avoid the pressures of competition.

Start collecting cents in a jar as a gift for your child's 18th birthday.

Learn to love broccoli, cabbage, or any other vegetables that you don't particularly enjoy. It's tricky to encourage children to "eat their greens" if they don't see you doing the same.

Rediscover the power of imagination and lose yourself in make-believe games; spend a day looking for fairies or chasing dragons.

Go somewhere special for a teddy bear's picnic, and turn an everyday outing into an adventure.

You don't need expensive toys to have fun with your child. Rediscovering the pleasures of simple games like "hide and seek," "eye spy," or even "it."

If your child has an imaginary friend, remain interested and ask questions rather than dismissing them —the power of make-believe is a beautiful thing.

Remind yourself how to use a
wooden sword and a fairy wand,
and prepare for the honor of
being your child's first playmate.

*Most small children love to
dress up, so collect bits and
bobs for a costume box from
charity stores or wherever you
can find them.*

Let your child loose with a box of face paints and have fun being whoever or whatever they want you to be for the day.

Start a treasure box of special objects that you can add to as your child grows and hand on to them when they are older.

Start collecting buttons, bows, ribbons, paper, and shiny things for impromptu art sessions. Salvage boxes from recycling and have fun junk-modeling.

Build your child a "den" and communicate with a "phone" made from two paper cups attached on a string. You'll both have fun and your child will feel a sense of independence in her special, secret place.

Look for possible dangers for newly mobile infants; sit on the floor to check out which cabinets, electrical sockets, and spaces seem inviting.

Be "naughty" together! Put on swimsuits when the sun comes out, and enjoy a water fight in the garden.

Buy the toys you secretly yearned for as a child on the premise that they're for your child when they are older!

THINGS TO DO NOW THAT YOU'RE...A MOM

Transform your house or garden into a magical playground and organize a treasure hunt with a small toy as the prize at the end.

Imagine your dream tree house and find a place in the garden to build one for your child.

Mastering the art of making your own play dough means there will always be something to do together on rainy days. There are plenty of recipes on line. Let your child choose the color.

Watch your favorite kids' movie with your child, then bring it to life and spend a day pretending to be the central characters.

Buy candy for trick-or-treating kids on Hallowe'en. Even if this custom annoyed you in the past, it won't be long before your little one will be out doing it, too.

Enjoy the opportunity to visit museums together. Many are free and most have a "hands-on" section, which allows you to play and learn with your child.

When planning a birthday party, keep your priorities clear! Parties are for kids, not for impressing other parents!

If snow falls in winter, wrap up warm and have fun showing your child how to make snow "angels" by lying down and waving your arms up and down.

Turn a floor-level cabinet into a "No Asking" cupboard and fill it with healthy snacks, crayons, and paper to nurture your child's growing sense of independence.

To ease any preschool worries, turn the idea of school into a game and set up a "classroom" at home for "teaching" teddies and dolls.

Hand over the shopping cart to your child and see what choices they will make for a meal. A little guidance will likely be required, but use it as an opportunity to teach your little one something about good food and healthy eating.

Give your children plenty of opportunity to cook—intervening or "helping" only with things that might be potentially dangerous or difficult to manage. Ignore odd shapes, textures, and tastes, and he'll be keen to repeat the experience.

Always take a moment to ask your child how school was— even if they claim they can't remember what they did, they will know that you care.

There might never be the "perfect" day to discuss changing bodies and sexuality. If you encourage an open dialog from an early age, these conversations will feel far less daunting as your child grows up.

If you can find the time, volunteering for an hour or so in your child's classroom is a great way to gain a better insight into their school life and environment.

Consider each birthday your child celebrates as the perfect time to see how much you can remember about your life, friends, and interests at that age. Not only will you gain greater awareness of the way they see the world, but you can also share priceless memories and experiences with your little one.

Making soups or salads together is a great way to encourage children to enjoy vegetables. Few children will fail to eat something they've made themselves.

Take time to discuss new boundaries together, as your child steps towards greater independence.
If they understand the reasons behind decisions they will probably have greater respect for them.

Spend a day on a beach or river helping your child to build dams and streams. If other children are nearby, invite them to join in. You'll experience purposeful industry that you've probably not felt for years.

Try to arrange a morning when your child comes to work with you, so they can begin to understand where you go and what you do each day.

On Valentine's Day, put a drop of red coloring in your child's milk——just to show her how much you love her!

Every now and then remind your child that you have a sense of humor and "break" an everyday rule. Why not try dancing on the table or starting a food fight?

Try reading a range of children's stories so that you can share thoughts and ideas about what they are reading.

One of every mom's biggest hopes is to be good friends with her children as they become teenagers and grow into adulthood. Strike a deal that you'll both remain open and honest, and try to honor that pledge without making judgments.

If you have had a disagreement with your child, leave a note on his pillow telling him how much you care. Record all the wonderful things you love about him.

It's great for your children to feel that they are better at some things than you are. If you've never learned to surf or skateboard, give it a go and give them the pleasure of feeling superior.

*Even if your child
pretends not to care, they
do look up to you. So try
to "walk your talk" and
be a positive role model
in all that you do.*

Turn your living room into a
movie theater—snuggle up
together under a duvet with
popcorn, ice cream, and a movie
that your child has chosen.

Often the simplest way to diffuse a difference of opinion with a child is gentle humor. Try to stand back and laugh at yourself in the hope that they will see the funny side too.

Special days out with an older child just get more and more fun. Book in for a spa day or take a trip go-karting.

Even when your child leaves home, they will cherish small gifts and mementoes that remind them of the time they spent growing up with you.

When the time comes for your child's first date, take time to reflect how much you've learned and grown since you were her age. Try not to tease; compassion and understanding will go a long way.

" Being a mother has made my life complete. "

DARCY BUSSELL

Stop—often—to congratulate yourself and celebrate your achievements as a mom.

An Hachette Livre UK Company

First published in Great Britain in 2008 by
Spruce, a division of Octopus Publishing Group Ltd
Endeavour House, 189 Shaftesbury Avenue
London WC2H 8JY
www.octopususa.com

Distributed in the US by
Hachette Book Group USA
237 Park Avenue
New York NY 10017 USA

Distributed in Canada by
Canadian Manda Group
165 Dufferin Street
Toronto, Ontario, Canada M6K 3H6

ISBN 13: 978-1-84601-288-4
ISBN 10: 1-84601-288-0

A CIP catalogue record of this book is available from the
British Library.

Printed and bound in China

10 9 8 7 6 5 4

This book contains the opinions and ideas of the author. It is intended
to provide helpful and informative material on the subjects addressed
in this book and is sold with the understanding that the author and
publisher are not engaged in rendering any kind of personal
professional services in this book. The author and publisher disclaim
all responsibility for any liability, loss or risk, personal or otherwise,
which is incurred as a consequence, directly or indirectly, of the use
and application of any of the contents of this book.